P9-EMP-290

THE OJIBWE

by Susan Stan

Illustrated by Luciano Lazzarino

ROURKE PUBLICATIONS, INC.

VERO BEACH, FLORIDA 32964

FRANKLIN PIERCE COLLEGE
LIBRARY
RINDGE, NEW HAMPSHIRE

CONTENTS

© 1989 by Rourke Publications, Inc.

All rights reserved. No part of this book may be reproduced or utilized in any form or by any means, electronic or mechanical including photocopying, recording, or by any information storage and retrieval system without permission in writing from the publisher.

Cover image of the bear and shield is the creation of the Ojibwe artist Jeffrey Chapman.

Library of Congress Cataloging-in-Publication Data

Stan, Susan.
  The Ojibwe / by Susan Stan.
    p. cm. —(Native American people)
  Includes index.
  Summary: Examines the history, traditional lifestyle, and current situation of the Ojibwe, also known as the Chippewa.
  1. Chippewa Indians—Juvenile literature. [1. Chippewa Indians. 2. Indians of North America.] I. Title. II. Series.
E99.C6S84 1989   970.004′97—dc19   88-24998
  ISBN 0-86625-381-5

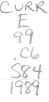
CURR
E
99
.C6
S84
1989

*Lake Itasca
in a serene wood.*
(Photo courtesy of Minnesota
Tourism Office)

INTRODUCTION

The Ojibwe, also known as the Chippewa, are the largest tribe of Native Americans north of Mexico. As many as 250,000 Ojibwe live in the U.S. and Canada. Their name is sometimes spelled Ojibwa, Odjibwa, Otchipwe, or Ojibway, which is how it is pronounced.

The name Chippewa, which sounds like Otchipwe, was bestowed by white men. It was first used by the U. S. government in treaties and is still used for official government business. Members of the tribe prefer Ojibwe or Anishinabe, an Ojibwe word that means "original people" or "spontaneous people."

The Ojibwe are a woodland tribe. They live in an area that stretches from the northern United States into southern Canada, surrounding the Great Lakes. In the U.S., Ojibwe live primarily in Michigan, Wisconsin, Minnesota, and North Dakota. In Canada, they live in Ontario and Manitoba.

For centuries before the arrival of the white man, the bountiful lakes and woods of North America provided the Ojibwe with everything they wanted. They lived in harmony with nature, taking only what they needed for food, shelter, clothing, and tools.

With the coming of Europeans to North America, the Ojibwe way of life changed. At first, as the Indians began to encounter French fur traders, the changes were relatively small. The Ojibwe hunters, who had before trapped only enough animals to provide food and clothing, now began to trap many more animals to sell to the traders.

Small changes gave way to larger ones, and eventually the Ojibwe found themselves forced onto reservations. They were no longer allowed to live how their ancestors lived.

Today the Ojibwe can live anywhere, and many live in cities and towns where they can find work. But if given a choice, most would probably prefer to live on the lands where their parents and grandparents grew up. There they could walk through the woods, fish in the lakes, and enjoy a special relationship with nature.

the Ojibwe

Canada

Great Lakes Region

U.S.A.

OJIBWE TERRITORY

LAKE SUPERIOR

LAKE HURON

LAKE MICHIGAN

LAKE ONTARIO

LAKE ERIE

ST. LAWRENCE RIVER

The Origin of the Ojibwe

THE CULTURE and history of the Ojibwe people have always been passed from one generation to the next through story-telling. During the winter, families used to gather around the fire and listen to stories told by the elders. Not many families still carry on this tradition, but some of the stories are now shared with Ojibwe children in other settings. Certain stories can only be told during the winter.

One important story tells of the creation of the earth by Nanabozho, called Wenabozho by some Ojibwe and Manabozhu by others. Nanabozho is an important figure in Ojibwe culture. A hero and trickster with special powers, he has cleverly outwitted nature's creatures when necessary and has helped the Ojibwe people. Nanabozho's name has many variations, as do most of the Ojibwe legends and stories.

In this variation, a huge flood covers the world. Nanabozho has climbed to the top of a pine tree, and he sees the other animals swimming around with no place to go. He asks them each in turn to dive under the water to bring up some earth. First the beaver tries, then the otter, and then the loon, but all three drown. The muskrat is the last to try; he, too, comes up dead, but with a small bit of mud and sand clutched in his paw. Nanabozho breathes on the muskrat and brings him back to life. Then he blows on the mud in his hands and enlarges it to the size of a small island. To make the island even bigger, he sends a bird around it. This he continues until the island is large enough for his aunts, uncles, cousins, grandparents, and the rest of the people.

Another important story explains how

the Ojibwe came to live where they did. Long ago, the Anishinabe lived on the shores of a great salt sea toward the rising sun (the Atlantic Ocean). In a sacred vision, the Megis, a beautiful glimmering seashell, rose out of the sea and appeared to the people. Its shiny surface caught the rays of the sun, providing warmth and light. The Megis instructed the people to move westward, and those who chose to follow the Megis packed up their belongings and began to travel west through the St. Lawrence Seaway to the Great Lakes region.

The whole journey took about five hundred years and included seven major stopping points. These stops often lasted for several generations, until the Megis apppeared again, causing the people to move on. At each stopping point, some members of the group decided to stay rather than continue with the journey. These people formed other tribes related to the Ojibwe.

The first major stopping point was at a turtle-shaped island in the St. Lawrence, near what is today the city of Montreal. The second major stopping point was Niagara Falls. It was during the time

spent here that the people first encountered Europeans. The third and fourth stopping points were along the Great Lakes, and the fifth stopping point was where the American and Canadian cities of Sault Ste. Marie would eventually be built. These two cities face each other across the St. Marys River, which connects Lake Huron with Lake Superior. The site of this stopping point would later become a major trading area between the Ojibwe and the non-Indian traders.

After this point, the Anishinabe split into two groups. Some took the northern route around Lake Superior and the others took the southern route. They met again at the western tip of Lake Superior, which was the sixth stopping point. Today Duluth, Minnesota, stands here. The last stopping point was at Madeline Island in Lake Superior. Here the Ojibwe found wild rice, which they recognized as the food that had been foretold to them in their oral traditions.

A related part of this story explains that the Anishinabe received their wisdom from the sun reflecting on the Megis during this long migration.

Traditional Life

The Ojibwe lived in bands of 300 to 400 people. The band was a loosely connected group of clans that lived in the same area. Each clan consisted of several families and had its own symbol, called a totem, or *dodem* in Ojibwe. Some common *dodems* were the catfish, the bear, and the wolf.

Each clan had a certain responsibility to the village. Some made canoes, while others were farmers or wood-gatherers. The function of certain clans was to govern. Membership in the clan was passed on through the father. When a couple married, though, they went to live with the wife's family for a few years.

In the village, the clans lived in dome-shaped wigwams positioned in a circle around a common area. The Ojibwe word *wigiwam* means dwelling. The wigwams consisted of a wooden frame of poles, bent and tied together with strings of basswood bark. Bulrushes or birch bark was stretched over this frame. The wigwam had a hole in the top to allow smoke to escape, and the door was covered with a hide or, in later years, a blanket.

Inside the wigwam, the fire was in the center, and each family member had a special place around it. The grandmother's place was on the side opposite the entrance. The mother's place was to one side of the entrance, and the father's place to the other side. Daughters were next to the mother, and sons next to the father. Children were taught to stay on their own side of the fire to respect the rights of the others as individuals.

The Seasons

With each new season, the Ojibwe moved to a different location to harvest the resources of the land. Families always returned to the same seasonal camps every year, and some left permanent buildings on the sites for annual use.

Summer

The summer village was situated along the shores of a lake or river. Every summer, families planted large gardens with potatoes, corn, beans, and squash. The women and girls gathered plants and herbs, which they used to make many different medicines. They also gathered wild berries — blueberries, strawberries, raspberries, and cranberries. The men fished, either with nets or by spearing the fish from canoes.

If they caught more fish than they could eat, they smoked the extras on racks over a low fire or strung them out to dry in the sun. They stored the smoked or dried fish away for later use. In some places, they also hunted deer and moose during the summer.

(Photo courtesy of Minnesota Historical Society)

Brown gold: finished wild rice.

Fall

In the fall, the band moved to the wild rice marshes to gather rice. They returned to the same location every year, and each clan had its own share of the rice field.

Wild rice was gathered from a canoe. One person poled the canoe through the marsh, while another person, seated in the stern of the canoe, bent down the stalks with one stick and used a second stick to knock off the rice kernels into the canoe. When the canoe was full of rice, they returned to shore.

The rice was spread out on birch bark to dry and then parched to loosen the husks. To remove the husks, the Ojibwe pounded the rice with long wooden sticks or stomped on it. They then winnowed the rice, separating the husks from the rice by tossing the rice in the air. The lightweight husks blew away while the heavier rice fell back into a tray. The rice was stored in bags woven of bark and sewed across the top.

Winter

After the wild rice harvest was finished, the Ojibwe moved to their winter homes in the forest. There they lived in wigwams that were longer than their summer homes. Winter wigwams, also domed, were usually long enough for two fires.

During the winter, the Ojibwe ate the food that they had stored and preserved during the other seasons. The men spent their days outdoors, hunting and trapping with bows and arrows, nets and snares, and later, guns and steel traps.

The women stayed inside, cooking the meat and preparing the animal hides. They made new clothing out of some hides, and saved some hides to trade. The women also made baskets, mats, bags, and many other items for household use.

During the long winter evenings, the elders told stories around the fire. The stories of the people were entertaining, and they also taught the Ojibwe many of the lessons of life.

(Photo courtesy of Minnesota Historical Society)

Collecting maple sap.

Spring

In late March or early April, the Ojibwe moved to the sugar bush, an area filled with sugar maple trees. Each clan had its own portion of the maple forests and set up camp nearby. Sugar time was a welcome relief from the hardships of winter and a chance for people to work and socialize together. It reinforced their special feeling of kinship and friendship.

Sugar makers drove a cedar chip into the tree and cut a gash right over the chip. Sap from the gash dripped down the chip and into small birch bark containers. These were emptied into large birch bark containers, where the Ojibwe cooked the sap by placing hot rocks in the containers. Later sugar makers used iron kettles, which could be set directly over the fire without burning.

After being boiled day and night, the sap thickened into syrup. Some syrup was used, but most was cooked longer and worked into granulated sugar. In this form, it could be stored and used throughout the rest of the year. Maple sugar was used to season fruits, wild rice, vegetables, and fish. Dissolved in water, it formed a cool summer drink, and it was also eaten as candy.

The legend of Nanabozho tells of the
creation of the world.

(Photo courtesy of Randy Croce)

Three dancers at White Earth wear colorful shawls.

Clothing

The Europeans brought cloth material and beads to North America. Before that, the Ojibwe had made all clothing out of leather and material woven from plants. They sewed pieces of leather together with animal sinew.

Women wore a sleeveless dress made of deer skin, belted at the waist. Ornaments usually hung from the belt. Under this dress a woman wore a woven skirt and leather leggings that came up above her knees. On her feet were moccasins. For extra warmth, she wore a fur robe over her dress.

Men wore a buckskin breech cloth, leggings that extended all the way up their legs, moccasins, and, in cold weather, a buckskin robe. Blankets eventually replaced the outer robes for men and for women. When cloth became available during the late 1600s, the Ojibwe began to use it instead of leather for both men's and women's clothing.

Shirts, dresses, and leggings were usually decorated in some way, often with porcupine quills that had been flattened and colored. They were sewn onto the leather with sinew. During the 1700s, glass beads replaced quillwork as a frequent form of decoration.

The Ojibwe acquired beads in trade from the early settlers. With them they created intricate floral designs on clothing and personal objects such as pouches, shoulder bags, and knife sheaths. Ribbons also became a popular form of decoration for clothing.

The eagle feather signified great personal bravery and was never worn merely as decoration. Only men and women who had undergone certain experiences were entitled to wear an eagle feather. The Ojibwe used color to paint their bodies, primarily the face. Some contemporary Ojibwe men still paint their faces for powwows.

(Photo courtesy of Minnesota Historical Society)

A birch bark canoe under construction.

Other Possessions

The Ojibwe found ample use for the wood and bark from the trees that surrounded them in the forest. They made dishes, spoons, bows and arrows, cradleboards, and many other every day necessities from wood and plants.

Birch bark was used to make all sorts of containers, from the small cups in which maple sap was gathered to the large containers used for cooking. Some containers were decorated with designs cut out of birch bark and sewed on with spruce root. On other containers, fancy designs were embroidered with porcupine quills.

Ojibwe canoes were also made of birch bark. Canoes were made in all sizes, depending on their use. Small two-person canoes to be used on rivers might be just 10 feet long. Large canoes built to carry 8 or 10 men on one of the Great Lakes were up to 40 feet long. Canoe makers first built a frame of white cedar strips, and over that they sewed the birch bark. Seams were sewn with tree roots and sealed with a gum made from boiling sap from the spruce tree.

Baskets were made of willow branches, sweet grass, basswood bark, cedar root, or wood splints.

(Photo courtesy of Minnesota Historical Society)

A grandmother and her daughter practice the art of basket weaving on Red Lake Reservation.

Above: A bag made of birch bark and sweet grass decorated with porcupine quills.
Left: A bandolier bag made of beadwork and cloth.

15

Values and Teaching

The Ojibwe culture cherishes children. The traditional way of bringing up children was gentle and yet instilled in them the values of the tribe.

Winters were often harsh, and infants and children were carefully tended so they would remain healthy. Couples usually had two children. Aunts, uncles, cousins, and grandparents all formed one close-knit family, and all often lived in the same wigwam. Aunts and uncles treated their nieces and nephews just like they treated their own children.

Children spent their first year on a cradleboard, securely bundled with their arms straight against their sides. This helped to keep babies' backs straight and made them feel secure. Mothers could easily carry the cradleboard on their backs or prop them up against the wall of a wigwam or a tree so that babies

A four month old baby in his cradleboard.
(Photo courtesy of Minnesota Historical Society)

16

could watch their mothers at work. A curved hoop at the top of the cradleboard protected the baby's head and was a good place to hang small charms and objects to amuse the baby.

Periodically during the day, the baby was taken off the cradleboard to get fresh air and exercise. From the time they were infants, children were taught to be quiet on command. A crying child could attract the enemy's attention if the family was trying to escape.

Children were brought up to respect and love other people and all living things. Sharing with others was important, and stealing and lying were forbidden and severely punished.

Children were taught to listen carefully when someone else, especially an elder, was speaking. It was by listening that one learned. If an Ojibwe child was scolded, he or she was expected to take the scolding and not talk back. Elders discouraged children from fighting with one another or taking sides in fights between others.

The women of the family taught the young girls how to cook, preserve foods, skin and tan hides, gather berries, and make wigwams and birch bark canoes. The men taught the young boys how to hunt and fish. It was important for everyone in the family to be useful; laziness was frowned on.

The Ojibwe believe that everything in life is a cycle. What they do for someone else, whether good or evil, will come back to them. If they share, then they will receive in their own time of need. This same belief also applies to nature and animals; if they feed a hungry animal or nurture a plant, these living things will repay them or another loved one someday.

Many of these values were taught to children through stories about woodland creatures who were too greedy to share or too lazy to work.

Early Contact with Whites

The first contact between an Ojibwe and a European probably took place at some point in the early 1600s. In 1640, French missionaries encountered Ojibwe summer camps in the Sault Ste. Marie area.

In their gradual movement west, the Ojibwe came upon other Indian tribes, often pushing them west or south. For the most part, the Ojibwe were on friendly terms with some of these tribes, such as the Fox in Wisconsin. Relationships with the Dakota (Sioux) tribe, though, alternated between peaceful and warring.

In 1679, the French explorer and fur trader Daniel Greysolon, Sieur de Luth (known as Duluth), helped the Ojibwe reach a trading agreement to act as middlemen between the Dakota and the French fur traders. The Ojibwe established a trading post in Grand Portage, located in what is now northern Minnesota. In the 1680s, Chequamegon, the Ojibwe village on Madeline Island, began to grow. By 1695 it was also a busy trading post for the Dakota and the fur traders.

By the 1720s, the French were expanding west, and they started trading directly with the Dakota. Trading at the Ojibwe posts declined, and relations between the Dakota and Ojibwe became strained. An incident in 1736 sparked a war between the two tribes that lasted for fifty years. During this time, Ojibwe bands moved often, affected by their war with the Dakota and encounters with other tribes and with white settlers and explorers.

The Leech Lake Ojibwe delegation to Washington, D.C. in 1899.
(Photo courtesy of Minnesota Historical Society)

Time of Treaties

Between 1837 and 1889, separate Ojibwe groups entered into nine treaties and three major legal agreements with the U.S. government, ceding their lands in Minnesota and Wisconsin. As historians have noted, these treaties and agreements laid the groundwork for contemporary Ojibwe life. They transferred most Ojibwe lands to non-Indians and established reservations for the Ojibwe. As a result, many of the traditional tribal ways were changed forever.

At the Treaty of 1937, held at Fort Snelling near what is now St. Paul, Minnesota, the Ojibwe ceded the pine forests in the St. Croix River valley and its tributaries, including most of their northwestern Wisconsin land. In return, they were supposed to receive annual sums of money and goods for 20 years. Some of the money was earmarked for farming and some for establishing blacksmith shops.

The Ojibwe were often bribed or badgered into signing treaties, and occasionally they were told that if they did not sign, the lands would be taken away from them anyway. Many of the Indians who signed believed they were giving whites right to use the land, not to own it. To the Ojibwe, ownership was a foreign idea. The land belonged to the Creator, who let them use it. Each time they took something from the land, they acknowledged it as a gift and repaid it with an offering.

With each new treaty, more lands became available to non-Indians. White settlers began moving onto the former Indian land. Michigan became a state in 1837, Wisconsin in 1848, and Minnesota in 1858.

(Photo courtesy of Minnesota Historical Society)

Chief Wadena, taken at the Mille Lacs Indian Reservation in 1925.

The Treaties of 1854 and 1855, made with Ojibwe in the Minnesota territory, were the first to set aside reserved lands for Indians in their own area. Until then, the Indian Removal Act passed by the U.S. government in 1830 had forced all Indians to move west of the Mississippi.

But as more white settlers came to the new state of Minnesota, even those reserved lands were called into question. The government began trying to consolidate the various groups of Ojibwe scattered around the state and move them all to one reservation. This was the purpose of the Treaty of 1867, which established the White Earth Reservation in northwestern Minnesota. Some groups, however, refused to move and stayed in their native area.

"Civilizing the Indians"

In 1887, the government passed the General Allotment Act. The commissioner of Indian affairs at the time said the act was designed "to break up reservations, destroy tribal relations, settle Indians upon their own homesteads, incorporate them into the national life, and deal with them not as nations or tribes or bands, but as individual citizens." The government's goal was to "civilize the Indians," or impose on them the systems of society and values that the Europeans had brought with them.

The Allotment Act divided reservations into 160-acre bundles of land — enough for a good-sized farm — and assigned a bundle to each man or head of family. In turn, these families were supposed to become farmers, following the lead of the European immigrants who had settled around them. Like the immigrants, the Indians were expected to "improve" the land by clearing the trees for farmland and building structures.

After the allotment process was complete, any leftover land was sold to non-Indians. In addition, much Indian-owned land was illegally taken away from individuals. Between 1887 and 1907, White Earth Reservation lost 80 percent of its land. The land the Ojibwes did retain was usually the most unsuited for commercial agriculture — the land that whites didn't want anyway.

(Photo courtesy of Minnesota Historical Society)

Major J.H. McLaughlin, inspector, U.S. Indian Department, visiting Mille Lacs Indians. He was trying to persuade them to move to White Earth Reservation.

(Photo courtesy of Minnesota Historical Society)

Signing of the Declaration of Allegiance to the United States at Leech Lake in 1913.

(Photo courtesy of Minnesota Historical Society)

Below: Totemic drawing by Ojibwe at Mille Lacs Lake, 1901.

(Photo courtesy of Minnesota Historical Society)

*Above: Chippewa woman
with child, about 1920.*

*Right: A fancy dancer
at Ni-Mi-Win in Duluth.*

(Photo courtesy of Randy Croce)

Boarding Schools

On the reservations, the Ojibwe could no longer live off the land as they had done for centuries past. Instead, they were dependent on the government for rations. In the late 1800s and early 1900s, many of the Ojibwe children living on reservations were ordered to attend mission schools far away from their families. Families who did not cooperate and send their children away were denied rations.

At the mission schools, Ojibwe children learned English and were forbidden to speak their own language. Their hair was cut, and they often wore uniforms. All traces of their own culture and religion were wiped out and replaced with Christian values. These children, some as young as five years old, attended class for half the day and did household and farm chores during the other half.

Sometimes these young children went for years without seeing their parents. By the time they were finally allowed to visit the reservation, many children had forgotten how to speak Ojibwe, and their parents, of course, did not speak English. Nonetheless, their reunions were filled with emotion.

In 1928, an official survey reported that Indian boarding schools were overcrowded and the children overworked and underfed. This study, the Meriam report, was a survey of Indian conditions requested by the government. Soon afterward, the government stopped forcing Indian children to attend boarding schools.

The Meriam report marked the beginning of many positive changes for the Ojibwe and other Indian tribes in the United States.

Reservations Today

The Indian Reorganization Act of 1934 followed the advice of the Meriam report. This important act ended the process of allotment. It also stated that any unsold land taken from the tribe by the Allotment Act should be returned and that money should be provided to repurchase the land that had been sold. This did not always happen. In addition, the 1934 act acknowledged the tribes' right to govern themselves.

Today the Ojibwe reservations in the U.S. are ruled by tribal government. The reservations have their own police force to enforce tribal law, and they issue separate license plates.

On the reservations, tribal programs and businesses employ as many people as possible. Sawmills and freeze-dried fishing bait companies make use of the reservations' resources. Ojibwe people on one reservation have begun to manufacture clothing. Marinas, campgrounds, and other tourist attractions, sometimes tribally owned, also provide jobs. The reservations have schools, daycare centers, medical clinics or hospitals, cultural centers, and other organizations that serve the community. Yet they still have high unemployment.

Not all Ojibwe live on reservation land. Many of the enrolled members of the Minnesota Chippewa Tribe, for instance, live in cities or towns in Minnesota. Many of these people were born elsewhere and have only visited the reservation with their parents or grandparents. Still, they often consider it home.

Important Dates in Ojibwe History

1525	Ojibwe arrive at their last stopping point on Madeline Island (approximate date).
1600s	First contact between Ojibwe and Europeans.
1679	Grand Portage Trading Post built; Ojibwe become middlemen between French traders and Dakota groups.
1736-1770s	Ojibwe-Dakota wars.
1824	U.S. creates Bureau of Indian Affairs.
1830	Indian Removal Act forces Indians to move west of Mississippi.
1837	Ojibwe cede lands in Michigan, Wisconsin, and Minnesota; Michigan becomes a state.
1848	Wisconsin becomes a state.
1854	First of two treaties (1854 and 1855) in which Ojibwe cede more lands and are moved to reservations.
1858	Minnesota becomes a state.
1867	White Earth Reservation formed in effort to consolidate Ojibwe and make more land available to settlers.
1887	General Allotment Act breaks up reservations and tries to destroy Indian culture.
1924	Citizenship Act makes Indians U.S. citizens.
1928	Meriam Report reveals government neglect of Indians.
1934	Indian Reorganization Act ends allotment.
1966	American Indian Movement (AIM) organized.
1972	Indian Education Act provides funds to meet educational needs of Indians on and off reservations.
1978	Indian Religious Freedom Act guarantees right to practice traditional religions.

INDEX

Much of the information in this book was first encountered in an excellent course on Ojibwe culture co-taught by Sally Hunter, a member of the White Earth Reservation, and Ona Whitebird, a member of the Red Lake Band. The author gratefully acknowledges their contribution and, in addition, the added consultation of Sally Hunter in the preparation of this book. Migwetch!